Crazy Curves

– Elisa Wilson –

Credits

Cover Design and Page Layout by Edd Hickingbottom

Printed in Canada by Friesens

10 9 8 7 6 5 4 3 2

Published by

Elisa's Backporch
1180 W La Entrada
Corrales, NM 87048
USA

www.backporchfabric.com

elisa@backporchdyeworks.com

Crazy Curves

ISBN 0-9745622-0-3

The heavens are telling of the glory of God;
And their expanse is declaring the work of His hands.

Psalm 19:1

Dedication

This book is dedicated to fellow "quiltaholics" who love to make, fondle and even just look at pictures of quilts. May your stash grow ever larger and your UFOs get completed.

To my husband of 20 years who is so supportive of me and what I do, even when there is no dinner on the table.

To my heavenly Father. If there be any good in me, if you see anything worthwhile, then to God be the glory.

Acknowledgments

Thank you to my family for doing without me during the deadlines. Thank you to Edd Hickingbottom who took my chicken scratch and made it look good and did it on a short time frame. Thank you to Linda Noort who took the time to quilt so many of these quilts and did such a good job and always on time. Thank you to Cindy Gamache who prayed for me and did lots of other work for me so I could work on this book. Thank you to Amy Varner for her input and suggestions. Thank you to Lori Paolino for contributing her creative ideas and quilts to be photographed.

Contents

hy the Drunkards Path?

The Drunkards Path as it has traditionally been known, is not a very glamorous name.

The basic Drunkards Path block is two pieces. It is a square with the arch of a circle separating it to make 2 pieces. The arch is 1/4 of a complete circle. If you put two of these blocks together you get a half circle. If you use four of them you get a complete circle.

Take a bunch of these blocks and put them together to create recognizable patterns like Rocky Road To Kansas or Robbing Peter to Pay Paul. The curves, when all patched back together, make a sort of "path". It is not very straight so possibly that is where the name came from.

Blue and white was a common color scheme used in making a Drunkards Path quilt. In the later part of the 19th century quilts were made using this pattern and were sold to raise money for the Women's Temperance Movement. Much can be said about the history of quilt making, the colors used and the political statements they represented. It is a fascinating topic. You can find more information and books to order at this web site; http://www.womenfolk.com.

Time marches forward and we continue to make quilts for a variety of reasons. I have my own theories on why we make more quilts than we can possibly sleep under. More on that later.

Why use the Drunkards Path shape? The curve is exciting. Think of roller coasters and wheels. All of them are curves. Curves represent movement. We make blocks that represent curves (the pinwheel and Storm at Sea) but usually we shy away from actually sewing with curves because we think they are too hard. Sewing with curves and adding lots of exciting colors makes for a very exciting quilt.

What you will find in this book

Take a look at the pictures of the quilts in this book. You will see a wide variety of styles and colors, all using the same basic block. Variations are added. Some look more complex than others. As you look at the pictures of the quilts, stop and examine the ones that you really like. Notice the main color or theme that attracts you. A lot of what attracts us to a particular quilt is the color. We are going to branch far away from what is know as traditional in color and use a lot of color or use color in different ways.

Some of the quilts will have the directions and fabric requirements given to make the quilt as shown. Not all of the quilts will have the fabric requirements. Some of the quilts are there to provide inspiration and get your creative juices flowing or for the joy of looking at the pictures. Because sometimes we can't see past the color choices shown, a smaller quilt can give you the picture of what those type of fabrics will look like put together. Some people want a complete recipe and others only need a few guidelines and they are off creating their own version. I hope to offer a little of both with the many varieties of styles shown. These are only a few of the ideas, many more are still dancing around in my head, waiting to be created.

The cutting and sewing directions are found in *Cutting Out the Pieces* and *Putting the Pieces Together*. Use those directions for the basis of all the patterns. I hope you will make one of the quilts as shown or become inspired to create something totally unique.

Lets get started and have some fun!

What's your favorite color?

I believe one of the major attractions to our obsession with quilting is our attraction to certain colors. Do you ever notice how a particular color makes your heart race or generates a certain amount of excitement. At least it causes a bit of commotion as bolts of fabric are rolled out to be cut and the Quilters gather around to get just a "piece" of the latest fabrics.

You have a color that you "love" and it hardly draws a sniffle from your best friend. When their favorite color is rolled out and they almost drool on the fabric. Have you ever been there? We are drawn to color like a butterfly is drawn to a flower. We like to be surround ourselves with our favorite colors. Sometimes we go in and fondle our stash of fabric. It sounds strange but this is a pretty harmless pastime.

You may have a passion for purple – any kind of purple, and your fellow quilter is delighted with blue. There is a color (sometimes more than one) that makes you want to create something. My personal favorite is green. I love it. It calls my name and I am drawn to it. I can sit looking at green fabric for hours, unable to choose a favorite.

Although green happens to be my favorite color, I don't want everything in my house to be green. That would be boring. In my bedroom I have some long swags over the windows in you guessed it – green but I have painted my walls a very soft peach. Not because I like peach but because it sets off the green.

So how do we go about choosing fabrics for your next quilt? The quilts using the basic 7" block are fun to make. Stay with the color(s) that you like but don't be afraid to branch out and experiment. Have some fun and you don't have to pick fabrics that are "just right".

I have two rules for choosing fabrics.

1 More important than the right color is the right *tone*

Tone is the intensity of the fabric. Some of the words you might use when describing the tone are; bright, muted, soft, dull, vibrant, pastel and so on. Take a look at the blue quilt on page 29 If you look closely the blues range from teal green to turquoise yellow and a few in-between. Some of the fabrics have bits of brown and yellow or green in them. They are the same intensity or tone so the colors work together. It is not so much about "matching" all the fabrics.

2 The more colors you use, the more colors you can have

Look at a scrap quilt. If you look closely at the individual fabrics. Most of those fabrics do not "match" or "go together" but because there are so many colors it allows your eye to travel around and you get an "over all" look to the quilt. If you were using only 3-5 colors in a quilt it would be more important that those colors worked together. Choose one that doesn't match and your quilt can look dreadful, or at the very least boring. Lots of colors allow your eye to move around and give the quilt an over all color scheme.

Once you have picked out a variety of at least 20 fabrics. Take a look at them and throw out any that are too dark or too light. Too much contrast can draw your eye instead of keeping the eye moving to get to over all look. Save those fabrics to use as an accent border.

These fabrics work well together but even though the light fabric "goes" with the others it is too light. It has too much contrast.

More suggestions include using a theme. A theme could be a grouping of fabrics from a particular company (like the Thimbleberries quilt on page 46 or the Benartex collection on page 37).

A type of fabric category could be Animal Skins or Oriental or Jungle or African or Hawaiian or Floral or Bright (dots, squiggles, stripes).

Work with a particular color – blues, greens, browns or pastels. Begin collecting your theme fabrics. If using pastels for example you can use blue, pink, yellow, green, or purple just as long as the tone or shade is pastel. When you visit quilt stores or the vendors at quilt shows and you see those lovely fat quarter packets and wonder what to do with them, now you know. Start working on your theme.

Did you notice that I haven't talked about the design or print on the fabric? I think the tone is more important than the design. But you should try to have a variety of small, medium and large prints along with some solids. This also adds variety.

Cutting out the Pieces

Templates are provided at the end of the book for you to cut out and use. I highly recommend you purchase the acrylic templates which will make this step go very quickly. You can use the order form or ask your local quilt shop.

With the invention of the rotary cutter the life of a quilter has been changed forever. The ease of cutting out pieces for our quilts is amazing. The alternative of tracing each piece and cutting out with scissors is very labor intensive.

The correct height of your cutting table and a sharp blade on your rotary cutter are of utmost importance. Adjusting your table to the right height not only saves your back and arms from extra stress but it helps keep your templates from slipping. I have added pieces of PVC pipe to the legs of my folding table to raise it about eight inches.

Press your fabric and lay it out on the cutting mat. You will most likely be working with fat quarters or other smaller pieces of fabrics.

I like to work near the end of my cutting table so that I can move around the table instead of moving the fabric and templates. Because you are cutting curves I recommend you layer only up to four layers of fabric at one time. A 45mm rotary cutter will work.

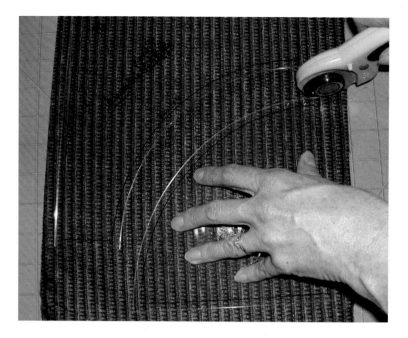

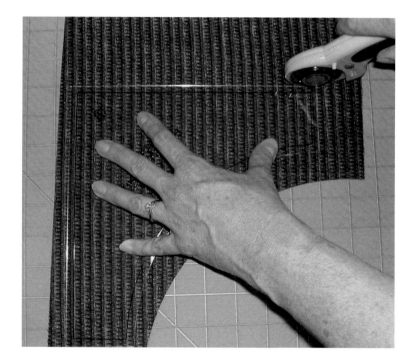

Place the rotary cutter next to the template and then cut. If you start cutting before you reach the template you risk nicking the template and dulling your blade. Cut the pie piece first and then the larger section. Cut carefully and keep fingers out of the way.

If using the paper templates, carefully trace around each shape on the wrong side of the fabric with chalk or a pencil and cut out with sharp scissors.

Putting the pieces together

hatever your experience with sewing curves, give this method a try and see how
easy and quickly you can piece curves.

Directions and pictures are given for the 7" template. This is the easiest to sew and it
is the one that I recommend you practice to learn how this technique works. Once you
know the technique and are comfortable with your ability to sew a decent curve you
can move on to the other sizes. The small 3 1/2" will be the most difficult.

 Fold each fabric to find the
center of the curve.

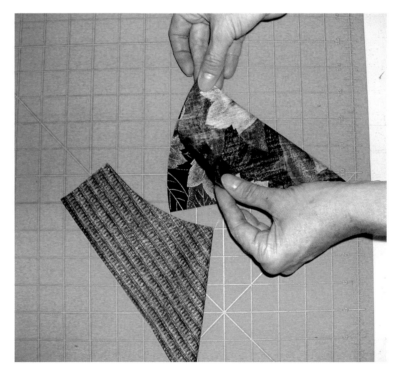

 Match these folds with the convex or pie shape on top. Place right sides together and pin.

 Align each end and pin 1/4" in from the edge.

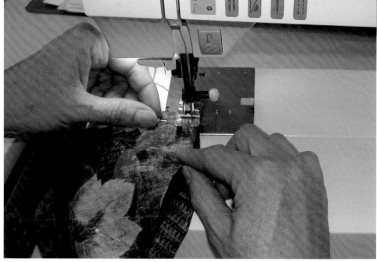

 Begin sewing.

USE A 1/4" SEAM ALLOWANCE.

Sew to the first pin. Leave your needle in the down position and remove the pin.

 Place your index finger of your right hand in-between the two pieces of fabric. This lifts the top fabric to reduce the friction and allows the two fabrics to align themselves. Slowly sew around the curve to the second pin. Do not stretch or pull the fabrics. Just align the edges and the curve will fall into place.

Stop at the center pin. Leave the needle in the down position and remove the pin. Place your index finger in-between the fabrics again and continue sewing half way around this second section of the curve.

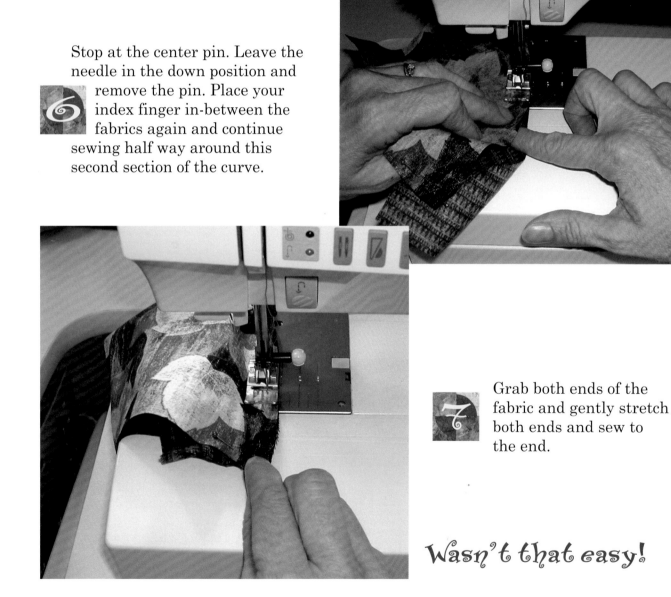

Grab both ends of the fabric and gently stretch both ends and sew to the end.

Wasn't that easy!

Take a look at your block. Did you keep your seam a consistent 1/4"? Do you have any tucks or puckers? Try another one and see how you improve.

If you have any problems with tucks it usually happens in-between the 2nd and 3rd pin. Try adding another pin in this location to prevent this. You are more likely to get tucks using batik or other tightly woven fabrics.

Flannel has more nap and usually more pins are needed.

Press the block gently from the back and then turn the block and press from the front. Your seam allowance can be pressed either up or down.

You do not have to bother with clipping the seams. They will lie flat in either direction. I usually press half of the seams up and half of them down. When I lay out all of my completed blocks some of the sides won't have a seam. If two seams are going in the same direction I re-press one in the opposite direction and sew.

If you are working with a two color quilt, press all the seams toward the darker color and they will all match up when sewing the blocks together.

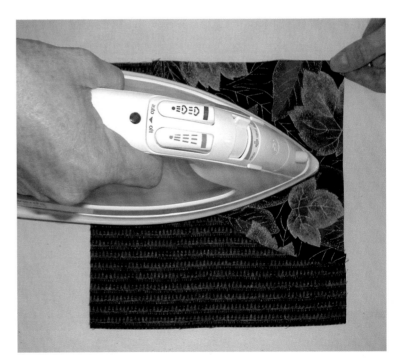

From Blocks to Quilt Top

fter you have

    1) chosen your color theme and

    2) cut out all of the fabric from the 20 or more fabrics.

You can sit down to sew. To begin I place the two different shapes in a stack and I randomly take from each stack. I only make sure that there is enough of a contrast between the fabrics so that you can see the curve. I don't try to figure out where each piece will end up in the quilt. Remember I already chose my fabrics and I know that they will work together.

hen choosing your 2 pieces, make sure there is enough contrast to be able to see the circle.

This is an example of good contrast

This is an example of poor contrast

The contrast here is okay. It could be used, but try for more contrast.

andomly sew the blocks and press them.

Then use your design board and lay out the blocks. This will probably be the hardest part. I place the blocks on the wall and turn them randomly until it looks pleasing to me. I start with making complete circles or play with only half circles. I make a pattern or leave it random. The hardest part is deciding when to stop and actually sew the blocks together.

I usually let the blocks sit on the design board for a few days and continually walk by it at different times of the day to see if anything jumps out at me. Then finally one day I just have to sew them together. Some people have commented on how "perfect the color placement is." If they only know how random it really is!

Quilting 101

This book is not designed to be a complete quilting manual for the beginner. There are many books on that topic. I will go over some of what I consider to be the most important of the basics.

To Wash or Not to Wash

Bring up this topic among experienced Quilters and you are likely to have a lively discussion. Some people have strong opinions and preferences. An excellent book that discusses this topic very well is *From Fiber to Fabric* by Harriet Hargrave. Upon reading that book you will learn that there isn't one right answer. It depends. It depends on your fabric and your water. If all of the fabric that you use bleeds, it could be your water. Also, bleeding fabric doesn't always mean that the excess dye is transferred to your other fabrics. Again it depends.

For most of my quilts I choose to press the fabrics with a steam iron before cutting. I like the look of a quilt when the fabrics and batting all shrink together. I use high quality fabrics and I have well water (no chlorine) and I use Synthraphol in the water. That is my answer to what I do.

The exception to this would be if I did a two color quilt using white and red. If I went to all of the trouble to have a two color quilt I would want to test and make sure I didn't end up with a one color quilt (pink!)

1/4" Seam Allowance

How many times have you read that in a book or pattern and your eyes glazed over and you jump to the next step. How many times have you actually checked to make sure your seam is correct? If you have trouble with consistent sized blocks – that may be your answer.

In some of my first quilts I started with a long piece of fabric and began sewing it to the end of my quilt. When I reached the end of the quilt I cut off the excess fabric. It was no wonder my edges looked like wings on a bat rather than a square quilt.

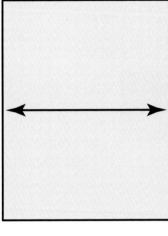

The way to measure for your borders is to measure across the center of the quilt. Cut two strips to this measurement. Match the center of this strip to the center of the quilt and pin. Then pin the ends. Yes, pin your borders. Ease in any differences and pin some more. Both sides will come out the same and any difference from side to side (which should be minimal if you used an accurate 1/4" seam) will be eased into the quilt.

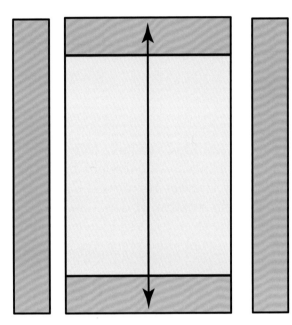

Take another measurement, this time including the borders that were sewn on and pressed. Cut two strips to this measurement. Again pin and sew.

Repeat these steps as you add more borders.

Squaring up blocks can be very important. Sometimes even under the best of circumstances blocks become askew. Use your square ruler and cut the block to make it square again.

I also like to square up the edges of my quilt after I add a border and before I add the binding. I keep squaring up every step of the way.

Quilting the Quilt

ne of the best books on quilting that I have found is *Machine Quilting Made Easy* by Maurine Noble. This is a good place to start to learn the basics and go beyond.

Free motion is my preferred method of quilting.
My words of wisdom on quilting are;

- Curved quilting lines help to make a quilt with straight lines in the block have movement.

- Straight lines quilted on a quilt with curves give more depth and movement.

- Variegated thread is awesome!
  On the following page are a couple of quilting ideas. Both are free motion and can be shrunk or enlarged to fit the size of the quilt blocks.

Here is a close up of Lori's quilting on her lonesome block quilts

Quilting Ideas

The Basic 7" Block Quilt

Basic quilt directions will give you the number of quilt blocks to make using a variety of fat quarters or two colors and includes a simple border. Use this as a guideline and add different borders to make it bigger or smaller or get creative and add more strips or use any combination of half-square triangles.

Double Size

Fabric Requirements

20 1/4 yards of fabric (fat or long) makes 80 blocks.

If using two colors you will want 2 1/2 yards each color.

Border Fabric Requirements

Inner border 1/2 yard
- Cut 6 strips 3"

Outer border 1 yard
- Cut 6 strips 5"

Quilt Measurements

Lay out the blocks in 8 rows of 10
- The top will measure 56" x 70"
- With basic border quilt will measure 70" x 84"

Different ways to arrange your blocks

Sample 1

Sample 2

More ideas for arranging the blocks

Sample 3

Sample 4

Sample 5

Sample 6

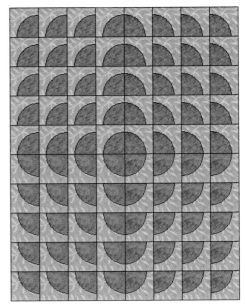

Sample 5 and 6 are actually the similar layouts, but sample 6 uses only two colors.

Crib Size

Fabric Requirements

8 fat quarters - makes 28 or 30 blocks.

If making a two color quilt you will want one yard of each color.

Border Fabric Requirements

Inner border 3/8 yard

• Cut 5 strips 2 1/2"

Outer border 2/3 yard

• Cut 5 strips 5"

Quilt Measurements

Lay out the blocks in 4 rows of 7

• Top will measure 28" x 49"

• With basic border quilt will measure 41" x 62"

Lay out the blocks in 5 rows of 6

• Top will measure 35" x 42"

• With basic border quilt will measure 48" x 55"

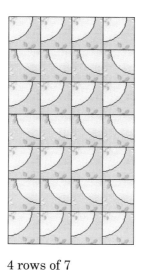

4 rows of 7

5 rows of 6

Quilts with borders

Twin Size

Fabric Requirements

17 fat quarters - makes 66 blocks.

If using two colors you will want 2 1/4 yards of each color.

Border Fabric Requirements

Inner border 1/2 yard

- Cut 6 strips 2 1/2"

Outer border 1 1/3 yard

- Cut 3 strips 5" for the top and bottom
- Cut 4 strips 7 1/2" wide for the sides.

Quilt Measurements

Lay out the blocks in 6 rows of 11

- Quilt measures 42" x 77"
- With basic border quilt will measure 56" x 87"

6 rows of 11

Quilt with border

Queen Size

Fabric Requirements

23 fat quarters – makes 90 blocks.

If using only two colors you will need 3 yards of each color.

Border Fabric Requirements

Inner border 1 yard

- Cut 8 strips 3 1/2"

Outer border 3 1/3 yards

- Cut 4 strips 15 1/2" for the top and bottom
- Cut 5 strips 12 1/2" for the sides.

Quilt Measurements

Lay out the blocks in 9 rows of 10

- Quilt measures 63" x 70"
- With basic border quilt will measure 93" x 108"

Quilt with border

King Size

Fabric Requirements

36 fat quarters – makes 144 blocks.

If using only two colors you will want 4 1/2 yards of each color.

Border Fabric Requirements

Inner border 1 yard

- Cut 8 strips 3 1/2"

Outer border 3 yards

- Cut 5 strips 12 1/2" for the top and bottom
- Cut 6 strips 6 1/2" for the sides.

Quilt Measurements

Lay out the blocks in 12 rows of 12

- Quilt measures 84" x 84"
- With basic border quilt measures 102" x 114"

Quilt with border

The Quilts

Basic Blue - using 7" template - Measures 67" x 82"
Machine pieced and quilted by Elisa Wilson

Notice the variety of blues used. A bit of brown and yellow adds interest. The inner border was folded together to make a narrow strip which I call an *accent border*. This makes the size of the quilt smaller.

A Hint of Africa - using 7" template - Measures 57" x 84"
Machine pieced by Elisa Wilson and machine quilted by Linda Noort. 2002.

The inner border was originally chosen to go in the quilt but it was too light but it makes an excellent fabric to border the blocks.

Batik Circle - using 7" template - Measures 62" x 75"
Machine pieced by Tammy Baldi and machine quilted by Linda Noort

A variety of batik fabric in "cool" colors was chosen for this bright quilt.

Untitled - Measures 55" x 55"
Machine pieced and machine quilted by Lori Paolino

A combination of plain 7 1/2" blocks were used with the 7" template block.

You don't always have to buy extra yardage for the back of your quilt. On the back of Lori's quilt she used batik fat quarters to make the back as exciting as the front!

Quick and easy project for baby

This quilt uses only 20 blocks. Dig out those scraps and start cutting.

Piece together 20 blocks. Sew them together in 4 rows of 5. Add a funky border and quilt with variegated thread. It couldn't be easier.

Quick and easy project for baby. Measures 43" x 37"

Oriental - Measures 66" x 81"
Machine pieced by Elisa Wilson and machine quilted by Linda Noort

Oriental was made using a collection of Asian type fabrics. Blocks were sewn together contrasting light and dark. The blocks were sewn into circles. Each circle was separated by sashing and the rows were staggered. Scraps were used for the border.

Adding Strata

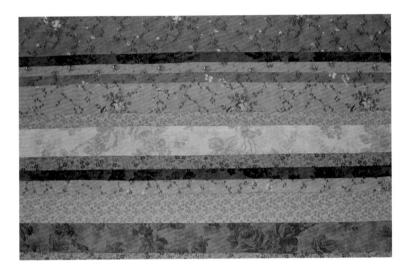

W̲hat's a strata?
– not a strudel –

A Strata is the plural of stratum. My paraphrase of Stratum is one of several parallel lines or layers. You could also think of them as rows.

Use your scraps and sew layers together. It is easier to use fat quarters when sewing strata. They are not as long so it makes pressing them easier.

Cut a variety of widths of strips. Don't cut them smaller than 1 1/4" or larger than 3". Sew the fabrics together in rows. Alternate the sizes of the strips and randomly place the colors. Press seams all in the same direction. It is easiest to press from the back and then turn over to press from the front.

Make strata about 24" to 36" wide. Don't make the strata too large or it is harder to handle. Make a couple groups of strata rather than one very large piece.

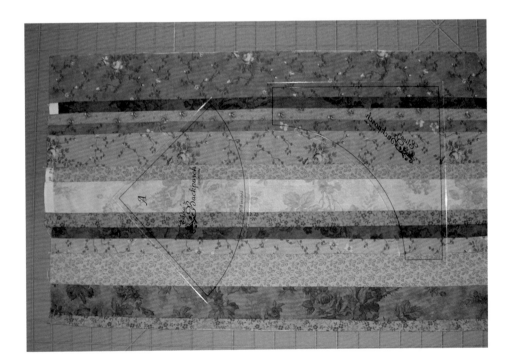

Lay out the strata on your cutting mat and use your template to cut out the pieces. Strata does not have to all go in one direction.

After your blocks are cut out you may choose to spray them with starch before pinning. Also, more pins will be needed. Take your time sewing around each curve.

Friends - Measures 72" x 78"
Machine pieced by Elisa Wilson and machine quilted by Leona Van Leeuwen

Friends was made from the True Friends fabric collection by Benartex. Strata was sewn together and half of the shapes were cut out from the strata.

Small Paths –
Pattern for 3 1/2" Quarter Circle Template

The steps for sewing the small block are the same as for the 7". I suggest you become familiar with sewing the 7" block before attempting the 3 1/2" block. The pieces are smaller and this can make it a bit awkward.

Fabric Requirements

- 20 - 1/8 yard cuts of fabric in a variety of colors.
- Optional – 1 yard of two different fabrics to make a two color quilt
- 1/4 yard for inner border
- 1/2 yard for outer border

 Cut 4 of each shape from each 1/8 yard of fabric. On some fabric you will be able to get more than 4 shapes. You will want at least 72 of each shape.

 Mix the colors and sew the shapes together. Make 72 blocks. Sew the blocks together in 8 rows of 9.

 Cut inner border into four 1" strips. Sew onto top.

 Cut outer border into four 2" strips. Sew onto top.

Makes a small wall hanging 41" x 41"
Machine pieced and quilted by Elisa Wilson

Using the 3 1/2" and 7" together

Four of the 3 1/2" blocks can be sewn together and used interchangeably with the 7" block.

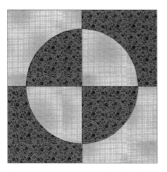

four 3 1/2" blocks

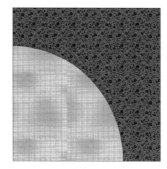

7" block

Quilt made in EQ5 using the 3 1/2" and 7" block

Sewing the 8" Block

The piecing is similar to the 7" and the 3" block but you will have an extra piece.

 Start with piece C & D. Fold each piece in half to find the center. Match centers, right sides together.
– Pin .

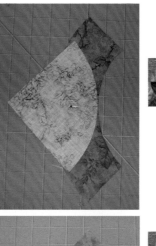

 Sew and press following the directions starting on page 12.

Fold this new piece to find the center. Fold piece B on the curve to find the center. Place right sides together. Pin and sew.

Completed block with arch.

Add corner block.
Draw a diagonal line on the wrong side of the 4" square of fabric. You may also press the fabric to find this line or use The Angler Two™!

Place square, right sides down in the corner.
Sew on the line.
Fold back fabric.

Press.

Cut off the extra corner pieces

Completed Block.

Lifesaver Quilt - Measures 48" x 48"
Machine pieced and quilted by Elisa Wilson

This was made from a packet of 16 fat quarters. Use steps 1-4 on page 41.

Tropical - Measures 67" x 67"
Machine pieced by Elisa Wilson and machine quilted by Linda Noort.

8" squares were used for the border. Use steps 1-4 on page 41. Fabric requirements are on the following page.

Fabric Requirements for Tropical

Arches

- 1/2 yard purple for the arch
- 1/2 yard lime green for the arch

Inner and Outer Circles

- 9 fat quarters

Inner Border

- 1/3 yard blue cut into 1 3/4" strips
- 1/3 yard green cut into 1 3/4" strips

Outer Border

- 1 yard green cut into 16 – 8" squares
- 1 yard blue cut into 16 – 8" squares

Sew 36 blocks. Make full circles alternating the purple and lime green arch. Sew the blocks together for the top. Sew the 1 3/4" strips together to make a wider strip. Sew onto the sides of the quilt. Add scraps for the corners.

Sew the purple and green 8" squares together, alternating colors. Sew a row of 7 blocks on each side of the quilt. Press. Sew a row of 9 blocks on the top and bottom.

Kaleidescope Circles - Measures 60" x 60"
Machine pieced and quilted by Lori Paolino

Various scraps of 3" strips were sewn together and cut out with piece C. Approximately 1 to 1 1/2 yards.

Other fabric needed:

- 9 fat quarters for pieces B & D

- 1/2 yard lime green for inner border – cut into 2 1/2" strips

- 1 yard for outer border – cut into 4 1/2" strips

Sew strata together from strips. Cut out 36 of piece C. Sew together using steps 1-4 on page 41. Add your inner and outer border as described on page 20.

Untitled - Measures 96" x 64"
Machine pieced and quilted by Elisa Wilson

This quilt was made entirely from a fat quarter packet of 35 fat quarters of Thimbleberries fabric. Use steps 1-9 on page 41.

More ideas from EQ using the 8" template

This design from EQ5 uses the pieces A and B from the 8" template set. A corner piece is added.

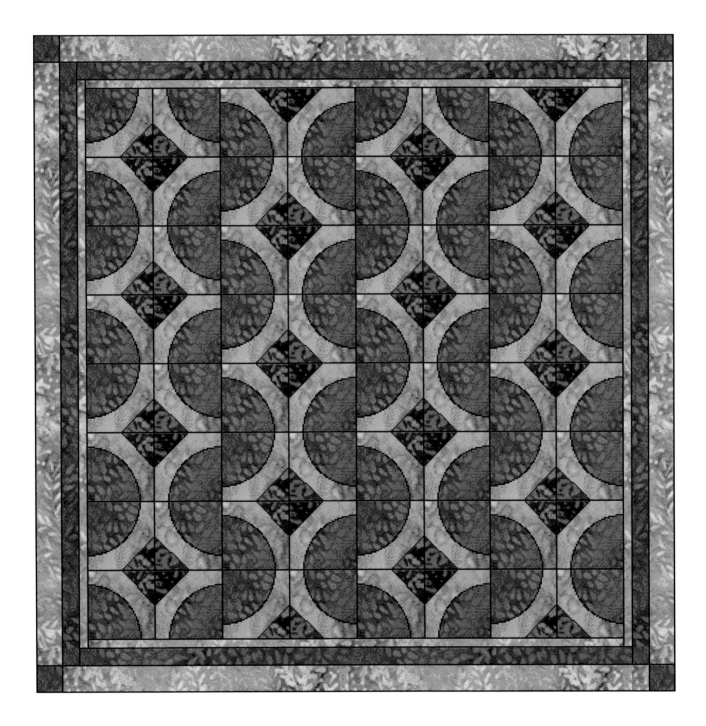

Watermelon Wedge

Fabric requirements

- Red -1 1/4 yard – cut 80 of pieces D
- Green - 2 yards – cut 80 pieces of C
- Yellow - 1 1/4 yard – cut 10 - 4 1/2" strips, sub-cut 80 - 4 1/2" squares
- Background – 4 yards – cut 80 pieces of 8" B
- 3/4 yard for binding – cut 11- 2 1/2" pieces

Border Fabric Requirements

- 3 yards for border – cut into 13" strips
- 1 yard for optional appliqué leaves on border - Use templates on pages 61 & 62

Quilt Measurements

Use the 8" finished sized template. Pieces B, C, and D

- The top will measure 64" x 80"
- With border quilt will measure 90" x 106"

Directions

Sew the blocks as shown on page 41. Press seams in towards the watermelon. Add the yellow corner piece.

Arrange the blocks in rows as desired. Sew the blocks together.

Piece together 13" border pieces and sew onto sides as shown on page 20. Press.

Sew 13" border onto top and bottom.

Cut out 30 or more of the leaves. Add seam allowance if you will be hand appliquéing the leaves. You can also use a lightweight fusible and machine appliqué or raw edge appliqué down the leaves.

The bias vines can be made by cutting 1/2" bias strips. Use the Clover fusible bias tape maker if desired.

Place appliqué leaves and vines in a random pattern or as desired.

Watermelon Wedge - Measures 90" x 106"
Machine pieced and quilted by Elisa Wilson

Machine or hand appliqué the optional grape leaves and vines.

Alternative ideas and ways to lay out your watermelon wedge blocks

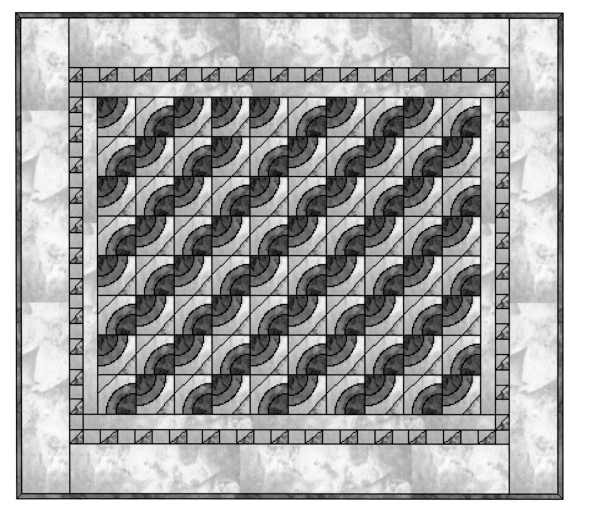

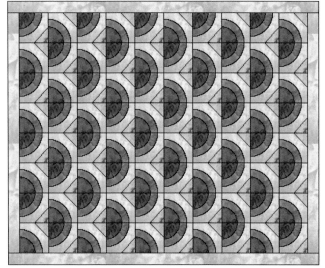

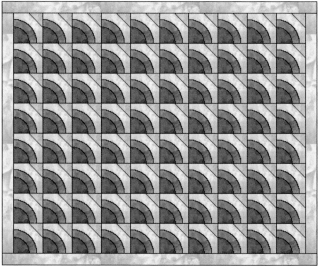

Determining Quilt Size

This chart shows the standard mattress size. The height of mattresses seems to vary a great deal.

- Be sure to measure the drop you want for each side of the quilt.

- Add this measurement to the mattress size to determine how big to make your quilt.

- Quilt batting is also approximate, depending on the manufacturer.

Standard Mattress Sizes

	Standard Mattress Size	Batting Size	Approximate Quilt Size
Crib	26" x 48"	46" x 60"	50" x 53"
Twin	39" x 75"	72" x 92"	65" x 88"
Double	54" x 75"	92" x 96"	80" x 88"
Queen	60" x 80"	92" x 108"	86" x 93"
King	78" x 80"	92" x 120"	104" x 93"

You might just get carried away making blocks and wonder what to do with the extras. Lori Paolino made these two fun quilts with her extra blocks.

- *Cut a 7 1/2" square*

- *Draw a diagonal line on the wrong side*

- *Place right sides together with a quarter circle block*

- *Sew 1/4" on each side of the line*

- *Cut apart on the line*

- *Press open*

You will have two new blocks.

Templates

The templates for the the projects in this book are here for you to trace The blue area is the finished size, and the green area is your 1/4" seam allowance. The templates are also available in easy-to-use acrylic. Use the order form in the back of the book to get yours.

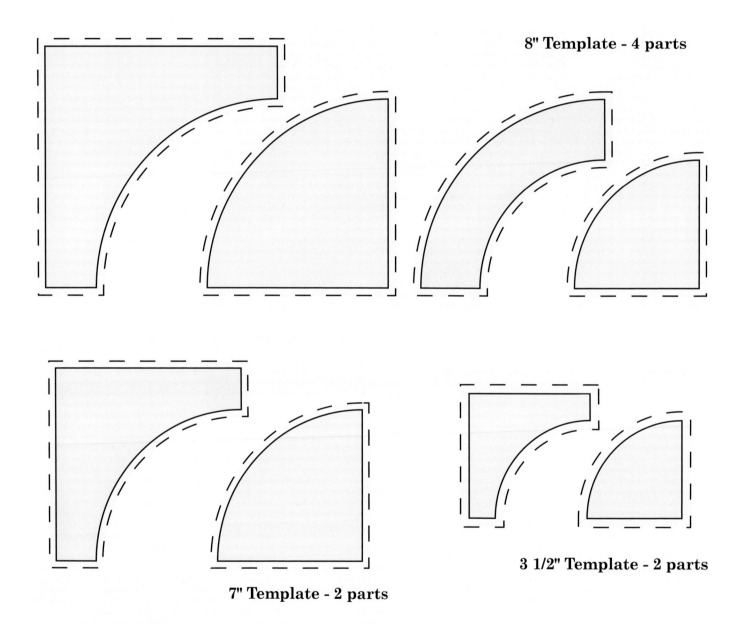

8" Template - 4 parts

7" Template - 2 parts

3 1/2" Template - 2 parts

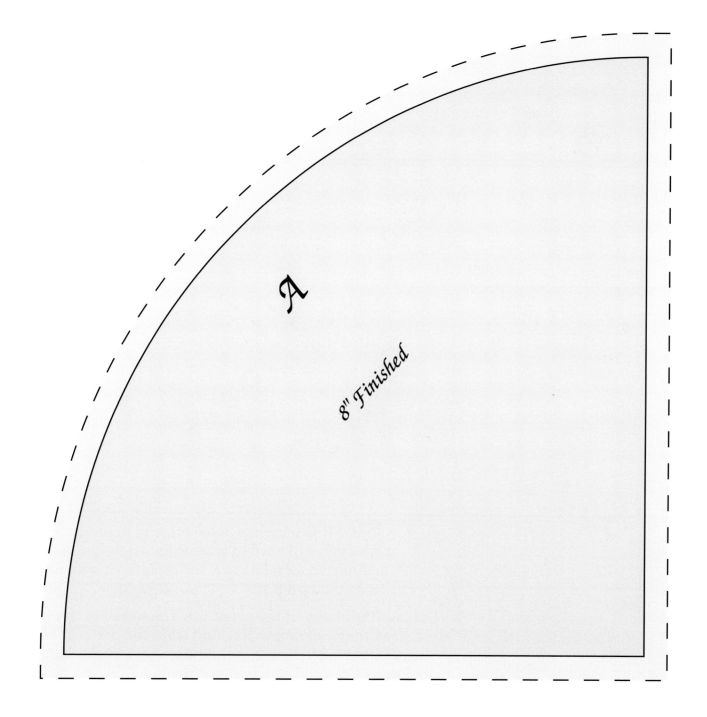

A

8" Finished

B

8" Finished

FOLD

FOLD

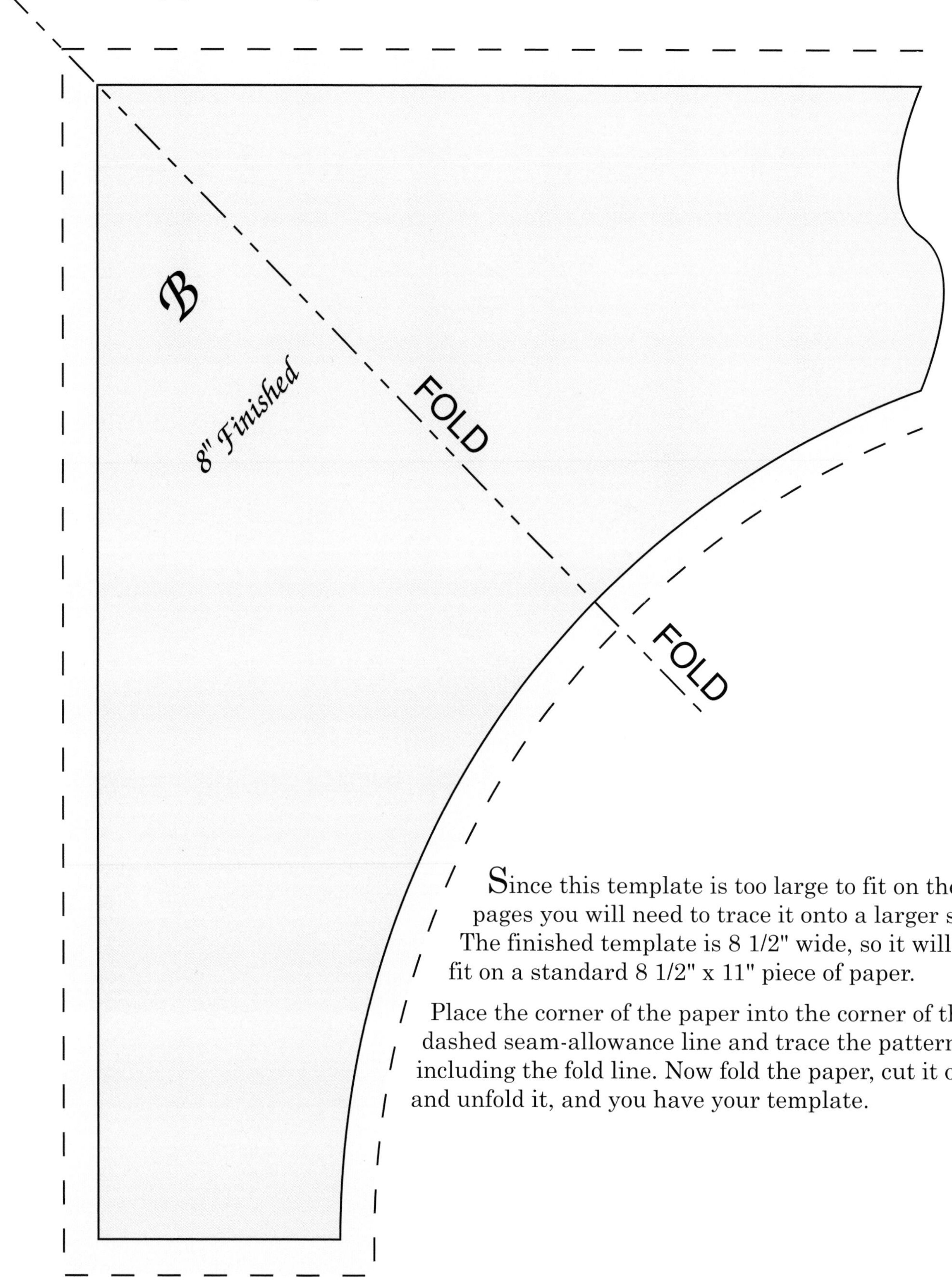

Since this template is too large to fit on these pages you will need to trace it onto a larger sheet. The finished template is 8 1/2" wide, so it will just fit on a standard 8 1/2" x 11" piece of paper.

Place the corner of the paper into the corner of the dashed seam-allowance line and trace the pattern, including the fold line. Now fold the paper, cut it out and unfold it, and you have your template.

8" Template - parts C and D

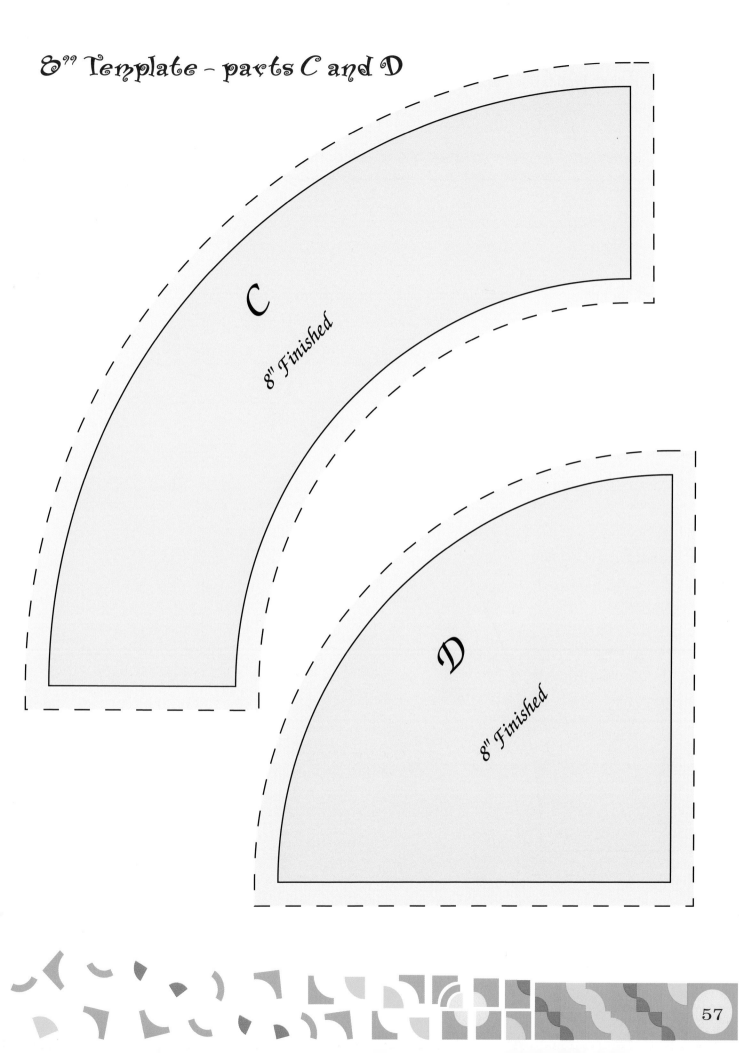

C

8" Finished

D

8" Finished

7" Template - part A

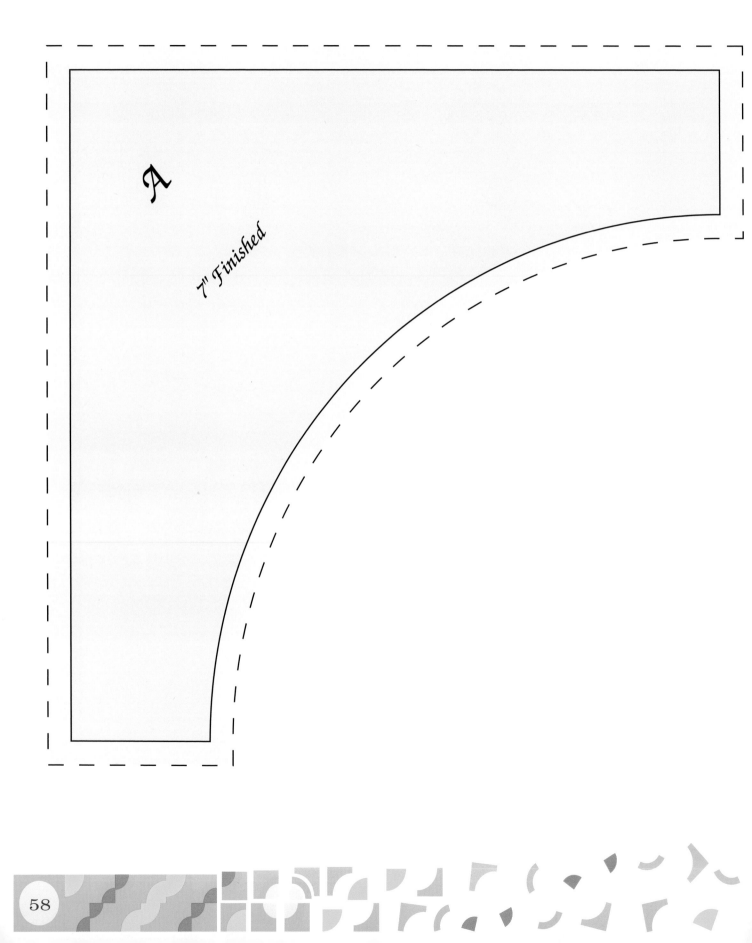

A

7" Finished

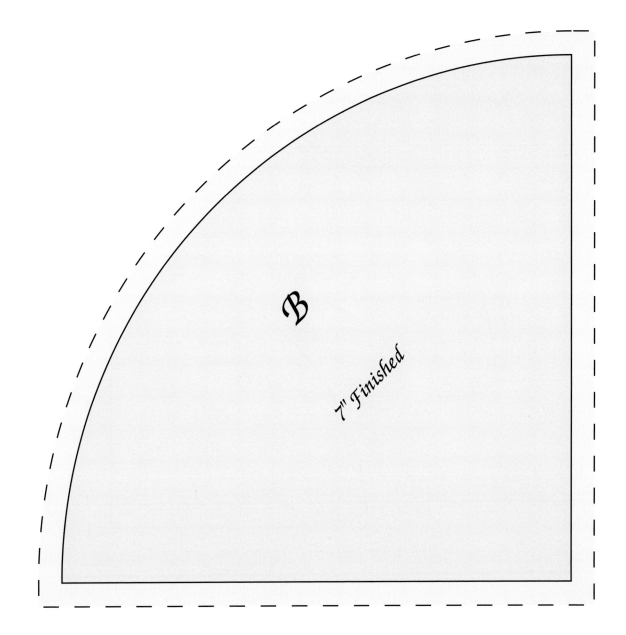

B

7" Finished

3 1/2" Template

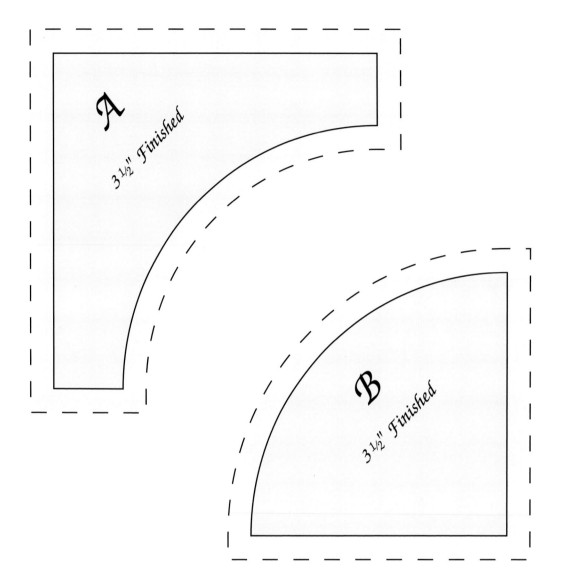

A

3 1/2" Finished

B

3 1/2" Finished

Leaves

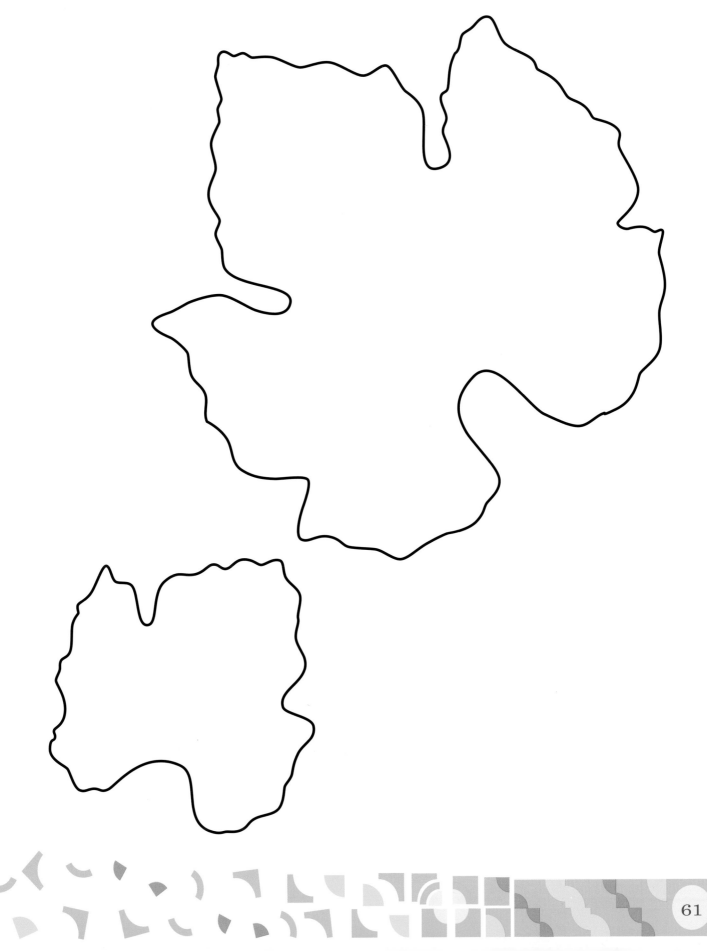

Leaves

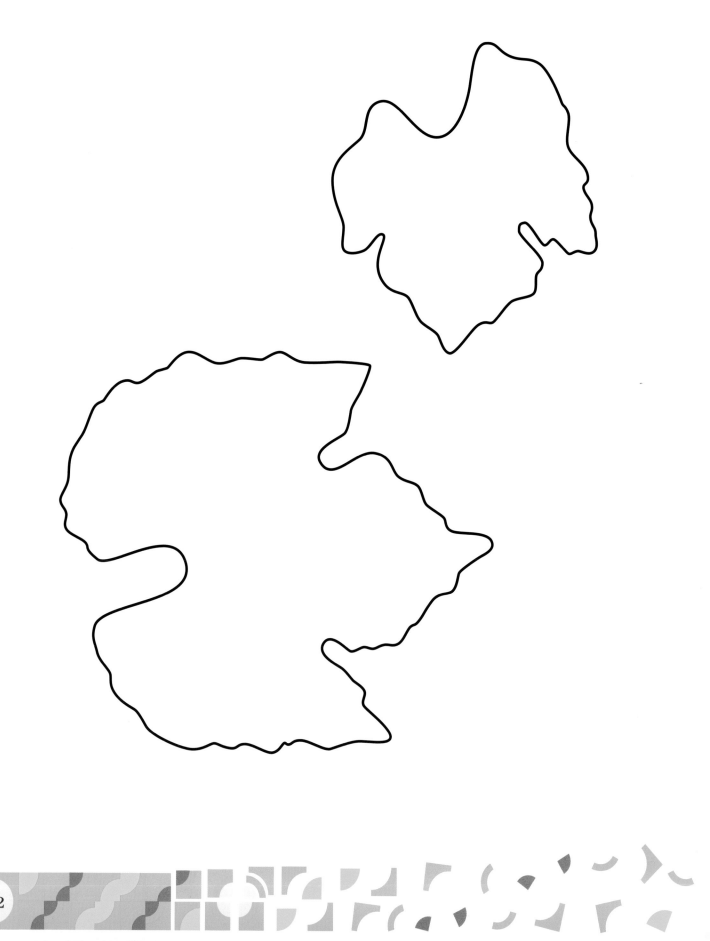

About the Author

I have been quilting "forever". The urge to make something has always been strong. I remember as a child making those brightly woven potholders – did anybody ever use those? I loved to knit and sew doll blankets. I don't remember how they turned out. It was the process that was the most fun.

I took Home Ec in 8th grade. I remember making a purple shirt. I had a difficult seam to sew over. For some reason this seam was very thick. I pushed the fabric through until it finally gave and the sewing machine needle went right through my thumb! That is an experience I will never forget.

When my children were small I began quilting in earnest. Some of my first projects were all hand pieced and hand quilted. It was easy to take small projects with me and sew while I visited with friends or the kids were playing in the park.

The desire to do it "different" has always been strong. Sometimes I read the directions but usually I changed them or wondered what it would look like if I did it differently. I have to admit that most of my projects didn't turn out as I had expected but the process was fun. I learned a lot.

I began to play with color. Sometimes with disastrous results. I remember working on a Double Irish Chain and I couldn't stick with the traditional color scheme. The quilt looked so horrible, I never did finish it. Years later I made a small Storm at Sea pattern and I couldn't just make the Storm at Sea blocks (which were difficult enough in my opinion) I had to change the color to "flow" across the quilt in a wave of lighter colors. It took a long time and that one turned out great. I began experimenting with scrap quilts and playing with the effect of dark and light fabrics.

In my early years of quilting I didn't have one single quilt in my house. I would have visitors come over and comment that they didn't see any quilts around but they knew I quilted. I gave them all away. I soon began to fill my house with quilts and haven't stopped yet.

Currently I live in New Mexico with my husband and best friend Don and my three teenage kids and one loveable dog.

Order Form

Date _____

Name _____

Address _____

City _____ State _____ Zip _____

Phone _____ email _____

Qty	Item	Cost	Total
	Crazy Curves Book	$21.95	
	7" Quarter Circle Template	$12.00	
	3 1/2" Quarter Circle Template	$9.95	
	8" Template four piece set	$21.95	
	Shipping		
	New Mexico Residents add 6.125% sales tax	Tax	

☐ Check   ☐ Charge

Credit Card # _____

Expiration Date _____ CVC # _____

Signature _____

SHIPPING

One Item $3.85

Two Items $4.95

$1.00 for each additional item

U.S. prices –
Call for out of country costs

Mail orders with payments to:

**Elisa's Backporch
1180 W La Entrada
Corrales, NM 87048**

(505) 897-1894 – Fax (505) 792-9371

www.backporchfabric.com

Email – Elisa@backporchdyeworks.com

Wholesale inquiries welcome at www.backporchdesign.com
Prices subject to change without notice

Crazy Curves Templates
Acrylic templates for rotary cutting – easy sewing directions

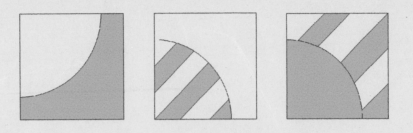

Two piece acrylic template set.
Makes a 7" finished block.
1/4" inch seam allowance included.

➤ Use the two pieces to make a traditional drunkards path block.
➤ Make a two-color quilt or pick at least 20 different colors for variety.
➤ Put the blocks together randomly to make circles and half circles.
➤ Place the blocks in a traditional setting.
➤ Sew strips together to add a stratum.
➤ Use the templates to easily cut out pieces from the strata.
➤ Strips for strata can be from 3/4" to 3" wide.
➤ *Crazy Curves* book will give you more ideas.
➤ See website for ordering information - www.backporchfabric.com

Elisa's
Backporch
1180 W La Entrada – Corrales, NM 87048
505-897-1894 – *www.backporchfabric.com*

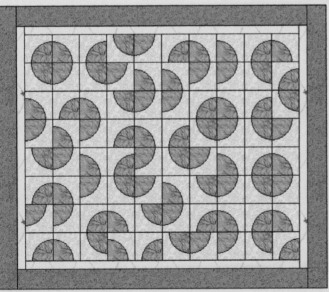

Suggested block layout for Crazy Curves Block

8 57238 00004 9

Crazy Curves Basic Block - 71" x 95" lap size quilt

◊ 20 quarters of fabric (fat or long) – 80 blocks
◊ Inner border – 1/2 yard
◊ Outer border – 1 1/2 yard
◊ Binding – 1/2 yard

Cutting – Use a 45mm rotary cutter with a sharp blade. Layer <u>up to</u> 4 pieces of fabric. Lay out both templates next to each other on the fabric. If you cut out the smaller convex curve first it allows more room to maneuver around the larger template, which has more angles. From a fat quarter or a long quarter you will get 4 of EACH shape, enough to make 4 blocks.

Use at least 20 fabrics in the "theme" of your choice. I like to cut out all of the pieces and then mix them up before sewing to get a wide variety of combinations in the blocks. As I sew the blocks together I don't try to "match" the fabrics but choose two fabrics that have enough contrast between the two to allow the curve to stand out.

Pin – Take a piece of each shape. Fold each fabric in half along the curve to find the center. Place fabric right sides together with the convex curve (pie shape) on the top, matching centers. Place a pin in the center. Align each end, pin about 1/4" in from each end.

Sewing – Use a 1/4" seam allowance. Take 3 or 4 stitches to the first pin, Keep needle in the down position, remove pin. Place your right index finger in-between the two layers of fabric. This lifts the top fabric and reduces the friction so that the pieces align as you sew around the curve. See to the middle pin. With needle in the down position, remove the middle pin. Realign and continue sewing half way around the remaining section. When you are about half way around, grab both pieces of fabric and gently stretch. Complete the curve by sewing around to the end. I like to do all of my pinning and chain piece the blocks.

*NOTE – if you are having any problems with the fabric "tucking" it will happen in-between the 2nd and 3ed pin. Place another pin in-between these two to prevent this. This is more likely to happen with batiks or other tightly woven fabrics that don't have much stretch. Your first block might seem a bit awkward but practice with a few more and you will be a pro in no time. No clipping of seam allowance is allowed or needed ☺
Gently press seam allowance from the back. You can press it up or down. Turn block over and press from the front.

Sew all of your blocks and place them on a design board or on the floor. Have fun turning them in different directions to create designs or patterns or leave them totally random. I let them set a day or so until I am happy with the arrangement. Sew the blocks into 8 rows of 10.

Cut the inner border fabric into six strips 2 1/2" wide. Piece together. Measure the width of the quilt. Measure in the center of the quilt. Cut two strips to this measurement. Pin and sew on. Press seams out. Measure again to get the length including the border strip you just sewed on. Cut two strips to this measurement. Pin and sew on. Press
Cut outer border fabric into six 6" strips. Sew on in the same manner as the inner border.